Galápagos Tortoises

by Conrad J. Storad

Lerner Publications Company • Minneapolis

For Sarah and Meghan. Teach my grandchildren to love and respect our world's creatures, large and small. —CJS

The images in this book are used with the permission of: © Thad Samuels Abell II/National Geographic/Getty Images, p. 4; © Laura Westlund/Independent Picture Service, p. 5; © Pete Oxford/Minden Pictures, p. 6; © Ken Lucas/Visuals Unlimited, p. 7; © iStockphoto.com/Mika Makelainen, p. 8; © Mark W. Kelley/Mira/drr.net, p. 9; © Martin Harvey/NHPA/Photoshot, pp. 10, 31; © David Hosking/Alamy, pp. 11, 22; © Jason Edwards/National Geographic/Getty Images, p. 12; © Larry Minden/ Minden Pictures/Getty Images, p. 13; © Ingo Arndt/Minden Pictures/Getty Images, p. 14; © Poelzer Wolfgang/Alamy, p. 15; © JTB/drr.net, p. 16; © Steve Winter/National Geographic/Getty Images, p. 17; © V1/drr.net, p. 18; © Jack Stein Grove/ Danita Delimont/drr.net, p. 19; © Craig Lovell/Stock Connection/drr.net, pp. 20, 48; © Jeff Greenberg/Art Directors & TRIP, p. 21; © Mark Jones/Danita Delmont Agency/drr.net, p. 23; © Tui De Roy/Minden Pictures/Getty Images, pp. 24, 36, 38, 43; © Hinze, K./Peter Arnold, Inc., p. 25; © Rosemary Clavert/Photographer's Choice RF/Getty Images, p. 26; © Michael Lustbader/drr.net, p. 27; © Tom Vezo/naturepl.com, p. 28; © David Cavagnaro/DRK PHOTO, p. 29; © Margaret Wilson/Peter Arnold, Inc., p. 30; Tui De Roy/Minden Pictures, p. 32; © Tom Oxford/naturepl.com, p. 33; © David M Dennis/Oxford Scientific/Photolibrary, p. 34; © ZSSD/ Minden Pictures/Getty Images, pp. 35, 37; © Martin Harvey/Peter Arnold, Inc., p. 39; © Wolfgang Kaehler/drr.net, p. 40; © David M. Dennis/Oxford Scientific/Photolibrary, p. 41; © Schultz, G/Peter Arnold, Inc., p. 42; © Mark Webb/Alamy, p. 46; © Tim Graham/Getty Images, p. 47.

Front cover: © iStockphoto.com/Mark Kostich.

Lerner Publications Company
A division of Lerner Publishing Group, Inc.
241 First Avenue North
Minneapolis, MN 55401 U.S.A.

Website address: www.lernerbooks.com

Library of Congress Cataloging-in-Publication Data

Storad, Conrad J.
    Galápagos tortoises / by Conrad J. Storad.
        p. cm. — (Early bird nature books)
    Includes index.
    ISBN 978–0–8225–9431–4 (lib. bdg. : alk. paper)
    1. Galápagos tortoise—Juvenile literature. I. Title.
QL666.C584S76 2009
597.92'46—dc22   2008025631

Manufactured in the United States of America
1 2 3 4 5 6 – BP – 14 13 12 11 10 09

Contents

PACIFIC OCEAN

ATLANTIC OCEAN

ECUADOR

N

area of inset

SOUTH AMERICA

GALÁPAGOS ISLANDS

Galápagos tortoises are found only on the Galápagos Islands in the Pacific Ocean off the coast of Ecuador. The red areas of the inset show where the tortoises live.

Be a Word Detective

Can you find these words as you read about the Galápagos tortoise's life? Be a detective and try to figure out what they mean. You can turn to the glossary on page 46 for help.

carapace	**hatch**	**predators**
climate	**hatchling**	**reptiles**
ectotherms	**herbivores**	**scales**
equator	**plastron**	**scutes**
extinct		

5

Chapter 1

Galápagos tortoises are giant tortoises. Where can they be found?

Living Giants

Giants still live on Earth. But there are not many left. To see one, you must visit a place called the Galápagos Islands. If you go, don't be afraid. The giants are only tortoises. But they are the biggest tortoises of all.

Tortoises look a lot like turtles. In fact, they are turtles that live on land. Both tortoises and turtles belong to a group of animals called reptiles. Lizards are reptiles. So are snakes and alligators. Tortoises and other reptiles have bodies that are covered with scales. Scales are flat, hard plates. They protect the reptile's skin.

Reptiles, like this caiman, have scaly skin. Tortoises are reptiles.

Tortoises have lived on Earth for a very long time. Tortoises are relatives of crocodiles and alligators. All of these animals were living here before the dinosaurs.

Galápagos tortoises are the biggest tortoises in the world. An adult male grows up to 6 feet long. That is as long as a dining room table.

Some animals, including crocodiles (above) *and tortoises, have lived on Earth since before the dinosaurs.*

Visitors to the Galápagos Islands can get up close to some tortoises. The tortoises are very big, but they are not dangerous to humans.

The biggest tortoises can weigh up to 600 pounds. That's as heavy as 10 second graders together. Female tortoises are smaller. They grow to about 300 pounds.

These Galápagos tortoises belong to a group called Geochelone nigra. *They have darker-colored shells.*

There are many kinds of Galápagos tortoises. All of them are huge. But each kind looks just a bit different. Some kinds have brown bodies. Others look black or gray.

The shape and length of their heads and necks are different too. So are the shapes of the tortoises' shells.

Galápagos tortoises have a range of colors, from brown to gray to black.

A tortoise's shell can enclose the animal's entire body. The tortoise pulls its head, legs, and tail inside its shell when danger is near. The shell is made of two layers. The hard upper layer is called the carapace (KAIR-ah-pays). The bottom layer is called the plastron.

A tortoise's hard shell provides protection for the animal. The tortoise pulls its head, legs, and tail inside the shell when it is in danger.

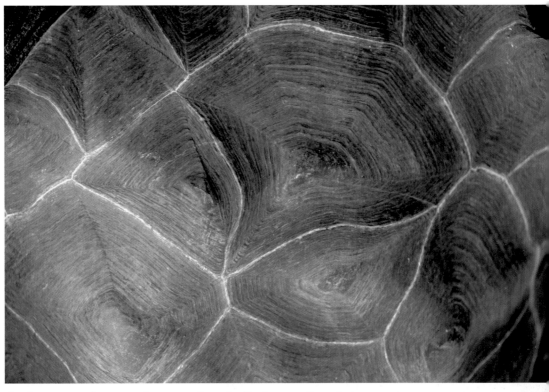

A close-up picture of a tortoise shell shows the plates of the carapace.

The carapace protects the animal from predators (PREH-duh-turz). It also provides shade on hot days. The outer layer of the carapace is made of plates called scutes (SKOOTS). Scutes are light and tough, like a person's fingernails. The inner layer of the carapace is made of hard bone.

Hard scales cover the legs of all Galápagos tortoises. The feet have toes and tough nails. Their feet are not webbed like turtle feet. Webbed feet help turtles swim. Instead, the front feet of tortoises have strong claws for digging.

A tortoise's tough legs are built for digging.

To lift itself off the ground, a tortoise's legs must be very strong.

A Galápagos tortoise's legs are thick and very strong. They look kind of like elephant legs. The legs must hold up the animal's heavy body and shell when it walks.

Galápagos tortoises walk with a slow, steady pace.

Galápagos tortoises are slow walkers. They are not built for racing or hunting. At top speed, they move about 0.2 miles per hour. That means that in one hour they can walk the length of three football fields. A third grader can walk the length of almost 53 football fields in that time.

Galápago is a Spanish word for "tortoise." When you say "Galápagos tortoise," you are actually saying "tortoise tortoise."

Chapter 2

The Galápagos Islands are near South America. What ocean are these islands in?

Island Life

Giant tortoises live a quiet life on the Galápagos Islands. The islands are in the Pacific Ocean, right on the equator (eh-KWAY-tuhr). The equator is an imaginary circle around the middle of Earth. It divides our planet in half.

The Galápagos Islands are west of the coast of South America. There are 13 large- and medium-sized islands and lots of tiny islands. The Galápagos tortoises live on the large and medium islands.

This photo was taken from the top of a volcano that created one of the Galápagos Islands.

Clouds and fog cover the mountains on the large islands. Meadows filled with juicy grass grow in these cool, wet areas.

Clouds and fog provide water to Isabela Island.
Plants there grow lush and green. Tortoises can find
plenty to eat.

South Plaza Island is a medium-size island. It is hot and dry. Plants like prickly pear cactus and red sesuvium grow well there.

The medium islands don't have high mountains. These islands get less water from clouds and fog. Plants that grow well in dry weather grow on the medium islands.

This tortoise warms up in the sun.

The Galápagos Islands have a wet season
and a dry season. But the climate (KLY-muht)
is still hot and dry for much of the year.
Galápagos tortoises have a special way of
adapting to the weather. They are ectotherms.

An ectotherm is a kind of animal. Its body temperature changes when the outside temperature changes. Ectotherms lie in the sun to warm up. If they get too hot, they move into the shade. Or they wallow in a mud puddle to cool down.

When tortoises get too hot, they cool off in a pool of water.

The hot, dry season on the Galápagos Islands lasts for many months. Few plants grow well when there is not much rain. It can be hard for Galápagos tortoises to find food. They are herbivores (ER-bih-vorz). This means that they eat plants. If there aren't enough plants to eat, tortoises will eat almost anything they can find. They eat dry grass and dead leaves. Sometimes they must eat the bodies of dead crabs to survive.

This Galápagos tortoise is lucky to find cactus to eat.

When water is available, tortoises fill up at ponds or puddles.

All the big tortoises store food as fat in their bodies. This helps them to live through the long dry season. The animals can live for a year without eating or drinking anything at all.

Chapter 3

This is a domed tortoise. Which types of islands do the tortoises with domed shells live on?

Dome or Saddleback

Some Galápagos tortoises have a high, domed shell. Other tortoises have a flat shell that looks like a saddle. This is called a saddleback shell. The tortoise's shell is a clue to where it lives. Why would this be?

It has to do with plants the tortoise can find to eat. Plants grow better on the bigger, wetter islands. A tortoise has lots to eat there and can grow big. Domed tortoises live on the large islands.

The large, wet islands have plenty of plants for tortoises to eat.

Domed tortoises feed on grass, leaves, and flowers. They also munch on fruits and water ferns that grow in ponds and puddles. Domed tortoises do not have to lift up their heads to eat. Plenty of food grows close to the ground on the biggest islands.

Domed tortoises can find lots of plants to eat on the ground.

The drier islands offer less to eat. Saddlebacks must be able to reach food wherever it can be found.

Saddleback tortoises live on the hot, dry, medium-size islands. Taller grass, trees, and spiny cactus plants grow on these islands. A tortoise has to stretch to reach the plants. A saddleback shell is raised at the front. The saddleback tortoise can lift its head and neck to reach and eat taller plants.

Saddleback tortoises are smaller than those with domed shells. But they have longer necks. They also have longer legs than domed tortoises. Saddlebacks are able to reach higher than domed tortoises can.

The saddleback tortoise's long neck helps it to reach plants that are higher off the ground.

The shell is attached to the animal's ribs. A tortoise cannot walk out of its shell.

Chapter 4

A baby tortoise can sit in the palm of a person's hand. How big was the egg it hatched from?

From Egg to Adult

Galápagos tortoises grow to be giants. But they don't start out large. A giant tortoise starts out as a round egg the size of a tennis ball.

Female tortoises will walk several miles to find the best places to make their nests. They look for dry, sandy ground. When they find a good spot, they dig a hole 12 inches deep.

Female Galápagos tortoises use their strong legs and claws to dig a hole for their eggs.

The mother tortoise will lay 2 to 20 hard-shelled eggs in the hole. Then she covers the hole and eggs with sand. The mother tortoise does not stay after she covers the eggs. She leaves to look for food. She does not return.

These eggs are kept at a research station in the Galápagos Islands. This will help protect the eggs until they are ready to hatch.

A baby tortoise breaks free from its shell.

It can take four to eight months
before the eggs are ready to hatch. The
weather is important for tortoise eggs. If
the temperature is cool, more male tortoises
will hatch from the eggs. If it is hot, more
females will hatch.

This baby tortoise is leaving its nest. Next, it must begin looking for food.

A baby tortoise is called a hatchling. It is only 3 inches long when it breaks out of its egg. Picture a small chocolate chip cookie with legs. The hatchling has to dig its way through the sand to the surface. Then the real work begins. The hatchling must find food and survive on its own. Its parents do not help it.

The hatchlings grow slowly. A two-year-old Galápagos tortoise is only about the size of a man's fist. It takes 40 years for the animal to reach full size.

Galápagos tortoises spend much of their lives alone. But these big reptiles do gather in groups when food and water are hard to find.

An adult tortoise stands next to a hatchling. It will take many years for the hatchling to grow that big.

Chapter 5

For a long time, Galápagos tortoises had no predators. Who became the first hunters of these tortoises?

Surviving the Future

Galápagos tortoises lived a quiet life for a long time. Food was plentiful. They had little to fear. No large predators lived on the islands. Most hatchlings grew into adults. At one time, there were 14 different kinds of giant tortoises. Hundreds of thousands of tortoises roamed the Galápagos Islands.

That changed about 300 years ago. That is when humans first visited the islands. Sailors and fishers stopped at the islands to get freshwater. They also needed food. They captured lots of tortoises and killed them for meat.

Only 11 kinds of Galápagos tortoises are still living. And many of these are in danger of dying out.

The humans also brought cows, goats, cats, and dogs with them. Cats and dogs dug up nests and destroyed tortoise eggs. They also ate hatchlings and young tortoises. Cows and goats crushed the soft carapaces of hatchlings with their hard hooves. Cows and goats also ate the grass and plants that the tortoises needed as food.

Tortoises compete with other animals for the food on their islands.

Baby tortoises are being protected at a tortoise breeding center on Isabela Island. Scientists hope this will help the tortoise population become strong again.

The Galápagos tortoises were almost all gone by 1959. There were fewer than 20,000 left. Some kinds were extinct (ehk-STINGT). An animal is extinct when none can be found living on Earth.

Many tourists visit the parks where Galápagos tortoises are protected.

The government of Ecuador (EHK-wuh-dor) stepped in to save the big reptiles. The Galápagos Islands belong to this South American country. Ecuador's government created Galápagos National Park. The park protects the places where the giant tortoises still live. People who visit the park must follow certain rules to make sure the tortoises stay safe.

There are fewer than 15,000 giant tortoises living on Earth. People have work to do. We must protect interesting animals and all the places where they live. The world would not be the same without Galápagos tortoises.

The oldest known Galápagos tortoise lived for 157 years. If people do their part, the tortoises will be around for centuries to come.

A NOTE TO ADULTS
ON SHARING A BOOK

When you share a book with a child, you show that reading is important. To get the most out of the experience, read in a comfortable, quiet place. Turn off the television and limit other distractions, such as telephone calls.

Be prepared to start slowly. Take turns reading parts of this book. Stop occasionally and discuss what you're reading. Talk about the photographs. If the child begins to lose interest, stop reading. When you pick up the book again, revisit the parts you have already read.

BE A VOCABULARY DETECTIVE

The word list on page 5 contains words that are important in understanding the topic of this book. Be word detectives and search for the words as you read the book together. Talk about what the words mean and how they are used in the sentence. Do any of these words have more than one meaning? You will find the words defined in a glossary on page 46.

WHAT ABOUT QUESTIONS?

Use questions to make sure the child understands the information in this book. Here are some suggestions:

What did this paragraph tell us? What does this picture show? Where do Galápagos tortoises live? What are two types of Galápagos tortoise shells? How long can a Galápagos tortoise live without food or water? What is your favorite part of the book? Why?

If the child has questions, don't hesitate to respond with questions of your own, such as What do *you* think? Why? What is it that you don't know? If the child can't remember certain facts, turn to the index.

INTRODUCING THE INDEX

The index helps readers find information without searching through the whole book. Turn to the index on page 48. Choose an entry such as *food*, and ask the child to use the index to find out what Galápagos tortoises eat. Repeat this exercise with as many entries as you like. Ask the child to point out the differences between an index and a glossary. (The index helps readers find information, while the glossary tells readers what words mean.)

LEARN MORE ABOUT
GALÁPAGOS TORTOISES

BOOKS

Heller, Ruth. *"Galápagos" Means "Tortoises."* San Francisco: Sierra Club Books for Children, 2003. The poems in this collection about animals of the Galápagos Islands are fun to read and full of facts.

Jacobs, Francine. *Lonesome George, the Giant Tortoise*. New York: Walker & Company, 2003. This is the story of George, believed to be the last giant tortoise of his kind. Find out about George and how scientists are still searching for more tortoises like him.

Mastorakis, Michael. *We're Off . . . to the Galápagos*. Chino Hills, CA: Cantemos, 2001. A nine-year-old boy wrote this book about animals of the Galápagos. The story is told in both Spanish and English words.

Rebman, Renee C. *Turtles and Tortoises*. New York: Benchmark Books, 2007. This book provides photos and information on animals in the turtle and tortoise family.

WEBSITES

Galápagos Conservation
http://www.gct.org
This site is dedicated to saving Galápagos tortoises and other wildlife.

Galápagos Islands
http:///www.pbs.org/safarchive/5_cool/galapagos/g22_geo.html
Here you can find out more about the volcanoes and other landforms of the Galápagos Islands.

Galápagos Tortoise
http://kids.nationalgeographic.com/Animals/CreatureFeature/Galapagos-tortoise
This site provides some fast facts about Galápagos tortoises.

Galápagos Tortoise
http://www.arkive.org/species/GES/reptiles/Geochelone_spp/
This site shows amazing photos and videos of Galápagos tortoises in their natural habitat.

GLOSSARY

carapace (KAIR-ah-pays): the upper shell of a tortoise or turtle

climate (KLY-muht): the usual weather of a place

ectotherms: animals whose body temperature changes when the outside temperature changes. Some people call ectotherms cold-blooded animals.

equator (eh-KWAY-tuhr): an imaginary circle around the middle of Earth

extinct (ehk-STINGT): when no members of a kind of plant or animal are still living on Earth

hatch: to come out of an egg. Galápagos tortoises hatch from eggs that are the size of a tennis ball.

hatchling: a baby tortoise

herbivores (ER-bih-vorz): animals that eat only plants

plastron: the bottom shell of a tortoise or turtle

predators (PREH-duh-turz): animals that hunt and eat other animals

reptiles: animals that have scales and that breathe air. Tortoises, turtles, lizards, snakes, and crocodiles are reptiles.

scales: flat, hard plates that protect a reptile's skin

scutes (SKOOTS): the plates on the outer layer of a tortoise's top shell. Scutes are tough like fingernails.

INDEX

Pages listed in **bold** type refer to photographs.